WOOSH

KA BOOM

TMP

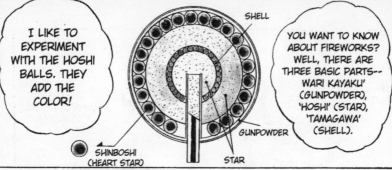

I LIKE TO EXPERIMENT WITH THE HOSHI BALLS. THEY ADD THE COLOR!

SHELL

YOU WANT TO KNOW ABOUT FIREWORKS? WELL, THERE ARE THREE BASIC PARTS-- 'WARI KAYAKU' (GUNPOWDER), 'HOSHI' (STAR), 'TAMAGAWA' (SHELL).

GUNPOWDER

SHINBOSHI (HEART STAR)

STAR

...

REALLY!?

I'LL GIVE YOU A PREVIEW OF MY NEWEST FIREWORKS!!

PRINCESS! COME TO MY HOUSE ON SUNDAY!

!

DING

I CAN'T WAIT FOR SUNDAY !!!

SUNDAY

...

KWEEK KWEEK ♪♫♪

HEY, RECCA.

SOMETHING HAPPENING TODAY?

TA

TA

TA

TA

DING-DONG

WHAT? NOW HE'S GOT GIRLS COMING OVER...

THAT'S HER!

THE PRINCESS IS COMING OVER !!

11

TOMP

TOMP

PERFECT FOR FIREWORKS!

THE SKIES ARE GONNA BE CLEAR TONIGHT!

IT'S A PIGPEN BUT COME ON IN!

PRINCESS!! WOW, YOU FOUND THE PLACE!!

I ONLY GOT LOST 12 TIMES.

SORRY IT'S SO DIRTY.

THIS IS MY ROOM.

KREEK

Ushio to Tora

ISBN4-09-123403-8
C9979 P3DE

MISS FUKO! MR. DOMON!

HEY GUYS. ♡

WHO SAID YOU COULD EAT THEM!?

MAN, I GOTTA SAY, THESE POTATO CHIPS ARE PRETTY DAMN GOOD!!

HEH HEH HEH HEH HEH

KRUNCH KRUNCH

YOUR DAD LET US IN. DIDN'T HE TELL YOU?

WHAT ARE YOU TWO DOING HERE!?

NATURAL BORN KILLERS

BANZAI BANZAI

NO, YOU CAN STAY.

MAYBE YOU TWO WANT BE ALONE?

HMM... ARE WE INTRUDING ON SOMETHING !?

UH...

SO MUCH NINJA EQUIPMENT AND BOOKS!

WOW!

IT'S CALLED "KUNAI" AND...

THIS IS A KŌGA NINJA-STYLE THROWING STAR.

SNS SNS

WSP WSP

YOU MUST BE OBSESSED.

OH! THAT'S A...

IS THIS A NINJA BOOK, RECCA !?

The Complete Manual Series
Everything you need to know about ninjas in one volume

IT'S MY DREAM!!

FWAP

OH.

Monthly
Loads of Busty Babes

Big Breasts are the Best

VOLUP-
TUOUS
CHIV-
ALRY

CHRIS-
TINA
OSHINO
(19)

HMM...

WHAK WHAK
SORRY
FWAP

HEY!! THAT'S NOT MINE!! I'VE NEVER SEEN THAT BEFORE!

SHAA
OOOO

ULP
!.....!

CHRIS-
TINA
OSHINO
(19)

B
U
N
G

SO
THIS IS
WHAT
RECCA
LIKES
...

FORGET THAT!

FUKO KIRISAWA!

DOMON ISHIJIMA!

IT'S TIME YOU ALL PROPERLY INTRODUCED YOURSELVES.

I'M THE SPUNKY CUTIE PIE! ♡

I'M THE STRONG, DEPENDABLE OLDER-BROTHER TYPE!!

YOU GO FIRST, DOMON!!

SWAP SWAP

OW! THAT'S MEAN AND RUDE!!

SHUT UP!

FWAK

YEAH, HE'S STRONG-SMELLING AND SHE'S A COW PIE!!!

I'M YANAGI SAKOSHITA!

I GUESS IT'S MY TURN.

YOU HAVE TO SEE IT!!

KLAK KLAK

ALL RIGHT THEN! I BROUGHT SOMETHING SPECIAL TODAY!

HE'S TURNING RED

LET'S JUST HAVE SOME FUN!

RELAX!

HAVING A BAD FEELING

PLAYSTATION? GAMEBOY?

WHAT IS IT?

THE OLD WOMAN PULLED THE BABY RECCA-MAN FROM THE RIVER.

A LONG TIME AGO, THERE LIVED AN OLD MAN AND AN OLD WOMAN.

WAAAH

Firestar ReccaMan
An Epic
(Peach Action)

by Rose Yanagi

RECCAMAN BEAT THE OGRES AND THEY ALL LIVED HAPPILY EVER AFTER.

TOGETHER WITH THE PHEASANT WHO CONTROLLED THE WIND, AND THE POWERFUL GORILLA HE MET ALONG THE WAY...

ONE DAY, RECCAMAN SAID:

RECCAMAN WAS A CHILD WITH THE POWER TO CREATE FLAMES.

I'M GOING TO SLAY THE OGRES.

ROAR

18

... THAT SUCKED ...

THE END

STORY BY ROSE YANAGI!

A-HEM

TAK TAK

Firestar
An Epic

A MASTERPIECE!

IT BROUGHT TEARS TO MY EYES!!

LOVED IT!! I-I LIKED THE POWERFUL GORILLA PART!!

KRAK KRAK

WANNA BE BURNT TOAST? SHE WORKED HARD ON THAT!!!

PLANET OF THE APES

YOU ARE A MONKEY

HOORAY

REALLY!? THEN I'LL WRITE ANOTHER ONE!!

YAY

LATER ...

THAT WAS FUN.

HE'S SHY, SO YOU'LL HAVE TO MAKE THE FIRST MOVE!

A BOY AND A GIRL WATCHING FIREWORKS. HOW ROMANTIC!

LATER, YANAGI!

GET 'IM, GIRL!!

WHAT!!?

BYE, YANAGI!! WE HAD FUN!

LET'S LEAVE THE LOVEBIRDS ALONE!

THERE IT GOES!!

NO...

I'M NOT WISHING FOR A BOYFRIEND.

OH.

THEY'LL PROBABLY END UP BEING A COUPLE QUICKER THAN US.

WHO KNOWS?

HOW 'BOUT THOSE TWO, FUKO?

I FEEL JUST LIKE CUPID.

RECCA IS ALWAYS WITH HER.

SO YOU'RE INTERESTED IN YANAGI SAKOSHITA...

WATER EXTINGUISHES FIRE.

YOU NEED TO DEFEAT RECCA TO GET CLOSE TO HER.

CAN YOU DEFEAT HIM, MIKAGAMI?

AND SO IT SHALL.

Part Eleven:
The Water Swordsman (1)
(Tokiya Mikagami)

Counselor's Office

JUNIOR, CLASS C, TOKIYA MIKAGAMI.

CLOSE YOUR MOUTH.

YOUR BREATH STINKS.

YOU'RE A STRONG CANDIDATE FOR A SCHOLARSHIP!

YOUR GRADES ARE VERY IMPRESSIVE!

IF ONLY THERE WERE MORE STUDENTS LIKE YOU.

I'M VERY PROUD OF YOU!!

HA HA HA HA

26

WITH THESE GRADES, EVEN TOKYO UNIVERSITY WOULD ACCEPT YOU!

WAIT, WE NEED TO DISCUSS YOUR FUTURE! WHAT ABOUT COLLEGE!?

EXCUSE ME.

WHAT DID YOU SAY?

NOT INTERESTED!? BUT YOUR *FUTURE!?*

I'M NOT INTERESTED.

I HAVE OTHER PRIORITIES.

IT'S NONE OF YOUR CONCERN.

WATCH OUT !!

MIKAGAMI !!

IT'S A SECRET. DON'T TELL ANYONE AT SCHOOL!

I'VE GOT A PART-TIME JOB.

I'M SORRY, RECCA, I'M GOING HOME ALONE TODAY.

PRINCESS WALKS HOME ALONE ONCE A WEEK.

C'MON KIDS! IT'S TIME FOR RECCAMAN!!

WHAT KIND OF JOB?

NURSERY SCHOOL !?

AKASAKA NURSERY SCHOOL

WH-WHAT !!?

WHAT'S RECCA-MAN DOING HERE !!?

33

YOU MUST REALLY LIKE KIDS.

BLOW.

HONK

OH NO, YOCCHAN! YOUR NOSE!

MISS SAKOSHITA!

OVER HERE, CHILDREN! ♡

YAAAAH

HA HA

IT TAKES A CHILD TO RELATE TO CHILDREN!

NOW I GET IT!!

HA HA

UH OH.

PLOSH

WAP

OOF!!

WAP

WAP

WHO WANTS TO WRESTLE RECCAMAN!?

CLIP: THE PEACHY SISTERS

LET'S PLAY MONSTERS!!

RECCA. YEAH YAY

OKAY, KIDDIES! STARTING TODAY, I'M YOUR NEW PLAYMATE!

YOU CAN'T HANDLE ALL OF THEM BY YOURSELF!!

I WANT TO BE PART OF THIS TOO, PRINCESS.

WAP WAP

RIGHT?

WHO YOU CALLIN' A KID?

I CAN'T REALLY COMMAND YOU BUT...

...

COMMAND ME AND I'LL HELP YOU WITH THESE KIDS!!...

YOU *ARE* MY MASTER, Y'KNOW!!

THANK YOU.

WHO I LOST ... LIKE MY BE-LOVED ... YOU LOOK JUST LIKE HER ...

AGAIN...

SO WE MEET...

SISTER.

RECCA HANABISHI.

HRASK

SEE YA, KIDDIES!

BYE RECCA!

OKAY. I'M OUTTA HERE!!

RECCA, I HAVE TO TALK TO THE HEADMASTER FOR A SECOND.

WATER

Part Twelve: The Water Swordsman (2)

(Water Sorcery)

HEY ...

NICE MANNER, BUDDY!

OOK

MONKEY!!?

LEARN TO TAKE CRITICISM... YOU'LL BE A BETTER MAN FOR IT.

THAT'S AN UGLY TEMPER YOU HAVE. ONE LITTLE INSULT SETS YOU OFF.

BUT HAVE YOU CONSIDERED HER FEELINGS, NINJA?

OR DO YOU CARE?

SELFISH FOOL!

YOU WANT TO BE A NINJA,

WILLING TO PROTECT YOUR MASTER WITH YOUR LIFE.

OR ELSE.

TAKE THAT BACK.

IS THE MONKEY ANGRY?

SOME NINJA.

FWOOM

I THOUGHT WE COULD TALK,

BUT THAT TIME HAS PASSED.

SEE HOW YOU ARE?

FWOOZ

TUMP

VWEE

I'M NOT THE SORT TO TURN THE OTHER CHEEK.

PLIP

PLIP PLIP PLIP

VWEE

EN

!!!?

PLURP

AAGH!

IT'S ...GONE !!?

!!

MY FLAME !?

ANY CHILD KNOWS THAT.

WATER EXTINGUISHES FIRE.

RECCA?

DID I...

I HEARD HIS VOICE!

AM I DREAMING?

...

AM I DREAMING?

UH, NOTHING. I'M FINE.

EH? WHAT'S WRONG, YANAGI!?

THIS DAGGER IS CALLED "ENSUI".

IT'S MY TREASURE.

ANY LIQUID, WATER, EVEN SULFURIC ACID, WILL TRANSFORM IT INTO A SWORD.

IT'S A GIFT FROM THE PERSON I LOVED MOST...

BUT I'M NOT REALLY INTERESTED IN YOU.

SHE WANTED US TO FIGHT.

I MET A LADY NAMED KAGEHOSHI.

THE DARK WOMAN IS RELENTLESS.

IT'S YANAGI SAKOSHITA I WANT ...

YANAGI'S IN DANGER AS LONG AS YOU'RE WITH HER.

SHE'LL NEVER STOP COMING AFTER YOU.

YOU UNDERSTAND, HANABISHI !!?

THAT WILL TRULY PROVE YOUR DESIRE TO PROTECT HER!!!

IF YOU CARE FOR HER, STAY AWAY FROM HER.

STOP THIS CHILDISH NINJA GAME!!

...BUT I...

...HANABISHI.

YOU SOUND LIKE A SELFISH CHILD...

PRINCESS !!! !!!

UNMISTAKABLY !!

THIS TIME I HEARD IT...

WHAT'S WRONG !!

THAT WAS RECCA'S VOICE !!

SOME-THING'S WRONG !

EEK !

IT FELT CLOSE BY!!

HE CAN'T BE TOO FAR ...

WUMP

RECCA !?

HE'S HURT BAD ...

WMP

I WAS WORRIED!

HUFF HUFF

YOU WERE FIGHTING AGAIN, WEREN'T YOU?

PRINCESS!!?

YOU'RE BACK, YOU'RE BACK!!

UNH...

I HEARD YOUR VOICE IN MY HEAD, RECCA!

IT WAS SO STRANGE! I HEARD YOUR VOICE!!

YANAGI'S IN DANGER AS LONG AS YOU'RE WITH HER.

IF YOU REALLY CARE ABOUT HER, STAY AWAY FROM HER!!

PRIN-CESS...

...

YOU'VE GOT TO STAY AWAY FROM ME.

YANAGI, LOOK...

WHAT
?

RECCA?

HE CALLED ME BY MY NAME... NOT PRINCESS.

THIS ...

IS AS IT SHOULD BE.

THE NEXT DAY

H-HEY
...

ARE YOU GOING TO PLAY WITH THE CHILDREN TODAY!?

HEY, RECCA !!

RECCA ?

DID I ...

DO SOMETHING TO MAKE YOU HATE ME?

CH UNK

BUT ...

K'R'K

SORRY ...

GRN CH

OF COURSE NOT.

I CAN'T BE YOUR SHINOBI ANYMORE!

I CAN'T BE YOUR SHINOBI ANYMORE!

TMP

DOES MEAN THAT...

I CAN'T BE WITH YOU?

PRINCESS!!!

YANAGI'S IN DANGER AS LONG AS YOU'RE WITH HER.

IF YOU REALLY CARE ABOUT HER, STAY AWAY FROM HER!!

Part Thirteen: The Water Swordsman (3) (Scolded)

THEY'RE HISTORY...?

IT'S OVER?

HE TOLD HER HE CAN'T HANG OUT WITH HER ANYMORE!

BLAB

BLAB

HANABISHI AND YANAGI ARE FINISHED!

NO WAY!?

WUNK

HEE HEE HEE

THEN MAYBE I SHOULD GO AFTER HANABISHI.

YOU LIKE HIM!?

TELL ME THAT STORY AGAIN.

TWO TICKETS... THEY EXPIRE TODAY...

Korakuen Amusement Park

Complimentary Ticket One Adult

SIGH ...

I WANTED TO GO WITH *HIM* ...

DID I DRIVE RECCA AWAY?

SKRK SKRK

BLURF

Korakuen Amusement Park

IT WON'T BE FUN IF I GO ALONE.

Complimentary Ticket

HR SSK

SNIFF

SNORK

1-F

HE'S FAILING IN HIS RESPONSIBILITIES AS CLASS CLOWN.

RECCA'S REALLY A MESS TODAY.

LET'S CHEER HIM UP!

HEY.

...

TAP TAP TAP

NO RESPONSE ... HMM ...

FSSS

THEN THE RUMORS ARE TRUE.

BONK

VEE EN

KLONK KLONK

NONE OF YOUR BUSINESS.

UH ...

THWAK

"MISAWA MITSUHARU ELBOW" !!!

WOOSH

BEING AROUND ME... PUTS HER IN DANGER.

HUH?

...

ERK

TALK OR LOSE TEETH !!

YANAGI'S MY FRIEND AND I'M MAKING IT MY BUSINESS !!

FWUMP

68

WHAT
!?

RECCA
...

!

IF YOU REALLY CARE ABOUT HER, STAY AWAY FROM HER..

TOKIYA
...

I HATE MYSELF.

FORGET ABOUT HIM..

I'M A JERK WHO BREAKS UP HAPPY COUPLES.

LET ME TAKE YOUR MIND OFF OF HIM....

HE'S NOTHING BUT PAIN.

DESPICABLE
...

IT'S FOR HER OWN GOOD.

BUT I CAN'T LET HER BE IN DANGER.

...ANOTHER TRAGEDY.

MY SISTER WILL NOT SUFFER...

BETTER TO BE A JERK THAN LET THAT HAPPEN.

WHAM

WHAT DID YOU WANT TO TELL ME, DOMON!

NOT MUCH.

IT'S ABOUT A COWARD WHO ABANDONED HIS FRIEND 'CAUSE HE LOST HIS NERVE!

JUST THOUGHT A CRAPPY NINJA LIKE YOU MIGHT LIKE TO HEAR A STORY.

YOU REALLY ARE CLUE-DEFICIENT!

SOMETHING ABOUT A COWARD?

YOU WANNA SAY THAT AGAIN!?

HA HA

WHAT'S WITH ALL THIS POUTING AND SOUL-SEARCHING!

CHARGE AHEAD LIKE YOU USUALLY DO, MORON!!

HA

GOOD THING HE DIDN'T TELL YOU TO KILL YOURSELF!

ARE YOU JUST GONNA SWALLOW WHAT HE FED YOU!? YOU'RE A DOCILE LITTLE LAMB, AREN'T YOU.

YOU GUYS ARE RIGHT!

DUMBASS!!

WHAT KIND OF A SHINOBI BREAKS HIS VOW?

I AM A DUMBASS!!

WHAT WAS I THINKING!?

THAT'S NOT HOW A SHINOBI BEHAVES!!!

I CAN'T CAVE IN SO EASILY!

AT LEAST HE'S BACK TO NORMAL.

HE'S NOT ONLY NAIVE, HE'S STUPID.

THEY'RE AT SOME AMUSEMENT PARK.

DOMON! FUKO! THANKS!!

DUH...

I'M SERIOUSLY INJURED HERE.

WE SHOULD FOLLOW HIM, DOMON!!

MY WOMAN'S INTUITION SAYS...

HE'S A LITTLE CREEPY...

I GUESS, BUT THAT TOKIYA GUY WORRIES ME.

TOKIYA MIKAGAMI ...

I JUST MET THIS PERSON ...

WHY AM I DOING THIS?

IT'S NOT RIGHT ...

Princess Yanagi

WANT SOME BREAD, RECCA?

What?

HAVE YOU SEEN THIS GIRL !?

HEY, MISTER !!

I'LL ASK AROUND!

GASP

....

Monster!?

NOOOO-OOOOO !!!!

UH-HUH.

WOB

ARE YOU OKAY ?

WHRRR

AUTHENTIC HAUNTED HOUSE

FEEEEEEER!!!!

WHEW

MISS YANAGI !?

WAAH !

PLOP

SHE'S SO DELICATE ...

82

THANKS, RECCA!!!

WOW.

SORRY, I DIDN'T THINK IT WOULD SCARE YOU SO MUCH.

!!

DON'T WORRY.

I JUST WISH IT HAD BEEN FOR ME.

THAT WAS THE FIRST TIME YOU'VE SMILED ALL DAY.

I'M ...

I'M SORRY ...

GASP

BECAUSE YOU REMIND ME OF SOMEONE.

MY OLDER SISTER MIFUYU. SHE WAS KILLED WHEN I WAS A CHILD.

SO WE CAN TALK.

Closed for the day.

The Labyrinth of Mirr

WE'VE GOT THE PLACE ALL TO OURSELVES.

WHERE ARE YOU, PRINCESS !!

HUF

HUF

DAMN !!

I'LL JUST HAVE CHECK IT ALL AGAIN.

THE HOUSE OF MIRRORS WAS CLOSED BUT I CHECKED EVERYWHERE ELSE.

SOUVENIR SHOP, ROLLER COASTER, MERRY GO ROUND...

GO TO *THE* LABYRINTH OF MIRRORS.

KAGEHOSHI?

THAT VOICE ...!!

WE WERE PASSED AROUND TO RELATIVES AND SHELTERS, BUT WE ALWAYS HAD EACH OTHER.

WE WERE A FAMILY OF FOUR. THEN OUR PARENTS DIED IN AN ACCIDENT.

AFTER SHE GRADUATED SHE GOT A JOB AND RAISED ME.

I ALWAYS HAD MY SISTER WITH ME.

SHE DID HER BEST. SHE WAS GOING TO PUT ME THROUGH COLLEGE.

SHE WOULD HOLD ME ON COLD NIGHTS.

BUT WE WERE HAPPY...

TIMES WERE TOUGH IN THAT OLD HOUSE...

UNTIL THAT TERRIBLE DAY.

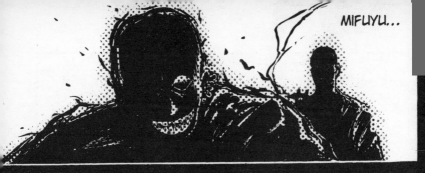

MIFUYU...

MIFUYU...

I'M SCARED.

LOOK OUT !!!

TOKIYA !!! !!!

I LIVE ONLY FOR REVENGE!!

THE PAIN ON MY SISTER'S FACE! THE PLEASURE IT GAVE THEM!!

CHING

I DIDN'T MEAN TO SCARE YOU.

I'M SORRY, FORGET WHAT I JUST SAID.

BA BUMP

BA BUMP

HE'S...

BA BUMP

YOU DID IT!?

YOU'RE THE REASON RECCA'S BEEN AVOIDING ME!

EVERYTHING'S ALL RIGHT NOW.

BUT HE WON'T ANYMORE.

MY HATRED DISAPPEARED FOR A MOMENT WHEN I FIRST SAW YOU.

AND... I COULDN'T ALLOW HANABISHI TO ENDANGER YOU!

92

...!

MY ...

...

YAY! YOU'RE TALKING TO ME AGAIN!

I'VE BEEN SO STUPID! FORGIVE ME!!

PRINCESS !!

YOU CUT PRINCESS'S HAIR? A GIRL'S HAIR?

KLAK

YOU DID THIS TO HER, TOKIYA!?

YOU DESERVE THE FIRES OF HEAVEN !!!

FASH

THE FLAME'S NOT THE SAME AS BEFORE...!!

!?

烈火の炎
～FLAME OF RECCA～

Part Fifteen:
The Water Swordsman (5)
(Water vs. Flame)

102

BUT LET ME KNOW LATER!!

OKAY ...

VERY TRICKY.

I GUESS YOU'RE NOT AS STUPID AS I THOUGHT.

HMM ...

SWISK

THERE WAS GUNPOWDER WITH YOUR FLAMES...THAT EXPLAINS THE EXPLOSION...

THAT IS NO LONGER NECESSARY ....

DON'T BE AFRAID... I'VE NO INTENTION OF HARMING YOU.

WHAT ARE YOU DOING HERE ?

WHAT ?

I HAD NO CHOICE ...

I DON'T KNOW IF YOU CAN BELIEVE ME, BUT I WANT YOU TO KNOW...

THE THINGS I'VE DONE WEREN'T MEANT TO CAUSE PAIN.

SHAOB

I'M SURPRISED YOU CAN EVEN STAND UP, HANABISHI.

BL URP

BL URP

HUFF

HUFF

HUFF

YOU CAN'T SMASH THROUGH MIRRORS WITHOUT GETTING CUT!

THE WOUNDS MAY BE SHALLOW, BUT YOU'RE LOSING BLOOD!! YOU COULD DIE.

FOR THE SAKE OF RECCA !!!

SVVK

I'M IN BAD SHAPE... AND MY FLAME IS GETTING WEAKER BY THE SECOND...

MAYBE I SHOULDN'T HAVE BEEN SO STUBBORN ...

WOBBLE

THIS IS NO GOOD.

OW ...

THUD

MIRROR !!

OH MAN ....

I SEE YOUR STUPID FACE EVERY-WHERE ....

YOU'RE THE STUPID ONE. CAN'T YOU TELL A REFLECTION IN A MIRROR FROM A HALLUCINATION?

WHAT?

TWO MORE.

TO AVENGE WHAT YOU DID TO PRINCESS'S HAIR!!

I'M GONNA BEAT YOU WITH TWO MORE FLAMES!!

BE CAUGHT UP IN SOMETHING UNEXPECTED.

RECCA WILL SOON...

THE ONE WHO CANNOT ESCAPE HIS FATE TO DO BATTLE...

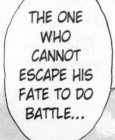

HE WILL ARRIVE!!

I'M GONNA BEAT YOU WITH TWO MORE FLAMES!!

Part Sixteen:
The Water Swordsman (6)
(Flames of Desperation)

TO BE HONEST...

I ONLY HAVE STRENGTH FOR TWO MORE...

TOKIYA MIKAGAMI, ENSUI, WIELDER OF THE WATER SWORD.

FLAMES OF DESPERATION

DAMN IT! I DON'T HAVE MUCH STRENGTH LEFT!

I WON'T EVEN BE ABLE TO MAKE SMOKE.

ONLY TWO MORE CHANCES! IF I FAIL...

AND HE'S TOUGH.

Part Sixteen: The Water Swordsman (6)

IF THAT HAPPENS, I'M ALL WASHED UP!!

116

HUH?

WHAT IS HE...!?

OH MAN!!!

CHOO CHOO

JUST ME AND FUKO ♡ AT AN AMUSEMENT PARK. HOW I'VE DREAMED OF THIS! ♡

THROB

THROB

TOO MANY PEOPLE!! WE'LL NEVER FIND RECCA IN THIS MOB!!

↑SIDE-PARTED MOHAWK

?

DUM-DEE-♪DUM

DUM-♪ DUM♪∞ DEE- DUM

HOW DELIGHTFUL...

IT'S CLOSED TODAY, MAYBE IT'S CONSTRUCTION.

OH! WHAT'S ALL THE NOISE COMING FROM THE HOUSE OF MIRRORS?

HUH?

PARDON ME, MISS FUKO, WOULD YOU CARE TO COME HERE AGAIN SOME TIME?

YUP!

RECCA.

I SHOULD HAVE KNOWN SHE'S NOT THE ROMANTIC TYPE.

NO WAY, I PREFER RACE TRACKS AND MAHJONG PARLORS.

DO YOU WANT TO DIE, HANABISHI !!!

YOU MUST BE OUT OF YOUR MIND!!!

I FINALLY GOT TO ATTACK! YOU LOOK LIKE YOU'RE IN PAIN TOO!

OW!!!

SH

YOU PLANNED THIS THE WHOLE TIME!?

YOU ...

ANYWAY, LET'S SETTLE THIS SOMEWHERE ELSE!

I DON'T WANT PRINCESS TO GET HURT.

!!

THE BLOOD ...!!

DA

!!

WH

KRAK-

WHERE'D HE GO?

HE'S GONE !?

K

!!!?

NOW FOR THE FINAL BLOW!

WAS I DECEIVED!? WHERE'S HIS REAL BODY?

MIRROR ...!!?

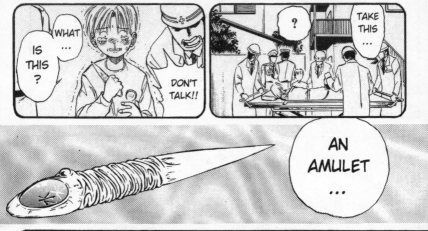

HOW CAN I AVENGE HER DEATH IF I CAN'T EVEN EXTINGUISH HIS FLAME!?

I HAVE TO WIN!!!

SHE'S WATCHING OVER ME...!

YOU SAID "WATER EXTINGUISHES FIRE."

TOKIYA.

THERE'S ANOTHER RESULT!!

BUT...

STEAM !!!

FIRE CAN TURN WATER TO VAPOR!!!

Part Seventeen:
Memories of a Dream

LOOKS LIKE IT'S ALL SETTLED.

HEY, THERE HE IS!! HANABISHI!!

TMP

I'M POOPED!

HANA...

IT'S NOT OVER, DOMON!

NOTHING'S SETTLED YET...

FwuF

SWIK

BUT NEXT TIME WE TANGLE, I'LL LEAVE YOU BALD!!

TSK TSK TSK TSK

I'LL LET YOU OFF WITH THAT!!

DON'T THINK IT CHANGES ANYTHING BETWEEN US!

I DON'T WANT YOUR MERCY!

I CAN'T STAY AWAY FROM HER!!

I'VE THOUGHT ABOUT THAT.

I'VE MADE UP MY MIND ABOUT THAT!

YOU SAID I PUT PRINCESS IN HARM'S WAY.

MUST COMMIT SEPPUKU!! (RITUAL SUICIDE)

A DISLOYAL SHINOBI, WHO FAILS TO PROTECT HIS MASTER...

IS HE FROM THE SENGOKU PERIOD OR SOMETHING?

HE'S SERIOUS...

HA HA HA

HEH HEH

YOU SWEAR TO THAT?

SWIR

AHAHAHAHAH!!

SWSH

RECCA HANABISHI.

HUFF

FINE BY ME.

THAT WON'T BE NECESSARY.

FOR NOW....

YOU'RE PUTTING YOUR LIFE ON THE LINE...

HANABISHI!!

RECCA!!

FWUMP

WAKE UP!!

SO I'LL BELIEVE YOU....

I'LL KILL YOU MYSELF IF ANYTHING HAPPENS TO HER!

CH!NK

IT'S A LONG SHOT... BUT I'LL TRY IT!!

THAT'S THE SAME AS MINE!!

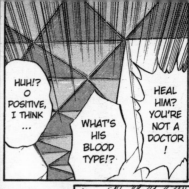

HUH!? O POSITIVE, I THINK ...

WHAT'S HIS BLOOD TYPE!?

HEAL HIM? YOU'RE NOT A DOCTOR!

SLISH

WHAT THE HELL ARE YOU DOING!?

STOP, DOMON !!

I HAVE THE ABILITY HEAL.

YANAGI... YOU...

LOOK.

THE WOUND...

SO I THOUGHT I COULD GIVE RECCA SOME OF MY BLOOD.

BUT...I CAN ONLY HEAL. I CAN'T REPLACE LOST BLOOD...

HEY, NOW THE TWO OF YOU ARE BOUND BY BLOOD!!

AMAZING! THEY SAY EVERYBODY'S GOT A GIFT...

HEE HEE ♡

LOVE IS STRONG, HUH, YANAGI? ♡

↑ RUDE.

YANAGI...

THE COLOR'S RETURNING TO HIS FACE!

HE SURE LOOKS STUPID LIKE THAT.

LOOK, FUKO... SHE'S RIGHT!!

TWINKLE

YES.

I LIKE RECCA A LOT!!

SIGH

A DECLARATION OF LOVE!!

AAAH!

N-NO! NOT LIKE THAT!

WHOOT! WHOOT!

OOPS

GA—SP

UH-OH.

WH-WHERE...

AAAAH!

I MEAN LIKE...YOU KNOW...LIKE A FRIEND.

I SAW HOW YOU LOOKED AT HIM!! WE WISH YOU TWO THE BEST.

WAIT A MINUTE.

WHERE ...AM I!?

EVERYTHING'S SO OLD FASHION...

LIKE AN OLD NINJA VILLAGE OR SOMETHING.

WHO ARE THEY?

HEY ...

IS THIS A DREAM?

INSTILL IN HIM EVERYTHING YOU ARE...

LIKE HIS OLDER BROTHER, KUREI, THIS PAGE IS A "CHILD OF FLAME."

IS THAT HIS MOTHER HOLDING HIM!?

A BABY! HE'S KINDA CUTE.

I UNDERSTAND.

THIS CHILD ...

WHAT'S HE TALKING ABOUT?

KAGERŌ ...

DO NOT LOSE.

WHATEVER HAPPENS FROM NOW ON...

RECCA ...

SAVE ME, RECCA ...

MY BELOVED SON!

AND ...

Part Eighteen:
A Glimmer of Light

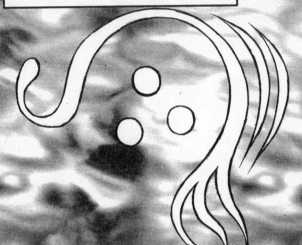

C-COM FOUNDATION DIRECTOR KŌRAN MORI WAS PRESENTED WITH AN AWARD.

FOR HIS DONATION TO CHILDREN'S SHELTERS ACROSS THE COUNTRY...

146

LISTEN TO YOU...

TAKE OFF THOSE SHADES! WHAT A SHOW-OFF.

FWAK

AW, SHUT UP AND GO TO SCHOOL!!

YOU HEAR WHAT YOU JUST SAID, HYPOCRITE!!

KRASH

I JUST FELT I HAD TO HELP OUT.

IT WASN'T FOR PUBLICITY.

HSSSSK

HMPH

TOLD ME SHE WAS MY FAMILY.

YESTERDAY THIS LADY...

HELP ME, MR. HANABISHI!!

SHEESH...

NAH...

COULDN'T BE...

HE'S STILL THE SAME KID.

YOU GUYS SEE TODAY'S PAPER!?

THE HOUSE OF MIRRORS IS IN THE PAPER!

DON'T BRAG ABOUT IT!! THAT WAS SENSELESS DESTRUCTION!!

YEAH, WE SURE BUSTED THAT PLACE UP!

YANAGI DOESN'T BELONG HERE EITHER!!

GEEZ, FUKO! DON'T JUST BARGE INTO OUR CLASSROOM, CRAZY!

LOOK AT THIS!

WE'RE LUCKY THE POLICE DECIDED NOT TO INVESTIGATE,

BUT IT SEEMS A LITTLE STRANGE.

IT'S WEIRD THOUGH, THEY CALLED IT AN ACCIDENT.

YOU BELIEVE IT, YANAGI?

RECCA LIKES TO STUDY?

I'M OFF ON A JOURNEY OF EDUCATION!!

DON'T THINK ABOUT IT TOO HARD!

1 - F

WHY'D YOU HAVE TO TURN INTO FOAM...

BOO-HOO

SOB

SNIFF

SNIFF

THE LITTLE MERMAID

SECOND PERIOD: MATH

F M W

HAYABUSA

POGO

HMM HMM HMMM

SKIRF SKIRF

FIRST PERIOD: ENGLISH

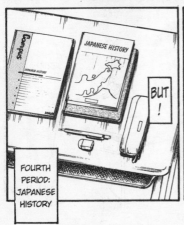

Campus

JAPANESE HISTORY

JAPANESE HISTORY

BUT!

FOURTH PERIOD: JAPANESE HISTORY

HE SAID, "I'M A BIRD!" AND LEFT.

HEY, WHERE'S HANABISHI?

HE'S YOUR TYPICAL SLACKER...

THIRD PERIOD: CONTEMPORARY JAPANESE

BECAUSE IT INCLUDES... NINJAS!

RECCA ACTUALLY ENJOYED JAPANESE HISTORY.

SWISK

TA-TA...

BUMP. BUMP

GROWR

SHUT UP! SHOW A LITTLE RESPECT FOR THE TEACHER!!

YOU CAN'T GET INTO A GOOD COLLEGE JUST BY STUDYING JAPANESE HISTORY, Y'KNOW.

HMPH

TRUMP

SO I'LL BE TEACHING JAPANESE HISTORY IN HER ABSENCE. MY NAME IS MR. TATESAKO!

HELLO, CLASS! MRS. TAMAKI IS ON MATERNITY LEAVE!

THAT'S NOT MRS. TAMAKI.

WHAT?

THANK YOU, BABY TAMAKI!!!

BECAUSE OF MRS. TAMAKI'S BLESSED EVENT, I GET TO MEET ALL OF YOU!!

ABSOLUTELY! NOW CAN WE TALK ABOUT NINJAS!!

IT WAS!?

NINJAS?

HILARIOUS!

YEAH!!

FWAK

EXCUSE ME...

THIS ONE MUST BE A KUNAI!

AMAZING, A FUMA CLAN SHOOTING STAR!!

RIGHT? RIGHT?

Faculty

PING

THEY'RE IN THEIR OWN WORLD.

IT'S UNUSUAL TO SEE HANABISHI IN HERE.

YEAH, AND YOU'RE NO SLOUCH YOURSELF!

HANABISHI!! YOU'RE QUITE THE NINJA EXPERT.

HEH

HEH

HEH

HEH

HI.

HEY, PRINCESS!

THERE'S SO MUCH MORE I WANTED TO TALK ABOUT.

IT'S TIME.

AS ONE NINJA FREAK TO ANOTHER, I HAVE SOME JUICY INFO!!

THIS IS GREAT!! NOT MANY PEOPLE ARE INTERESTED IN NINJA THESE DAYS!!

152

COME TO MY PLACE AFTER SCHOOL!!

THERE'S A GROUP OF NINJAS THAT WILL OVERTURN COMMON BELIEF!!

COOL...

HAHA HA.

THAT'S RIGHT!!

COMMON BELIEF?

OVER-TURN?

WOW...

DON'T BE SHY, COME ON IN!!

DRAGGED ALONG

154

NOW FOR THE REALLY GOOD STUFF!

EVER HEAR OF THE HOKAGE NINJA CLAN?

HANABISHI...

THEY'RE ALMOST A LEGEND...

DON'T FEEL BAD, HARDLY ANYONE'S HEARD OF THEM. THEY'RE NOT MENTIONED IN HISTORY.

NOT QUITE. THAT'S YAGYU TAJIMA'S SECRET YAGYU CLAN.

A COMBINATION OF FUMA NINJA AND SHIN-EI-RYU KENPO?

THEY COULD RUN ACROSS TWO MOUNTAINS IN A SINGLE NIGHT, THEIR SPEED WAS LIKE THE WIND! THEY FLEW THROUGH THE SKY AND WALK THE OCEAN!!

AS YOU KNOW, NINJAS WERE AGILE, SKILLED ASSASSINS, EXPERTS WITH SHURIKENS, KATANAS, AND EXPLOSIVES.

LEGEND...

FWUP

BUT THE HOKAGE NINJAS WERE DIFFERENT !!!

WH AM

THIS !

THEY DIDN'T HAVE MANY SPECIAL ABILITIES--

THEY WERE AVERAGE RUNNERS, MEDIOCRE SWORDSMEN ...

BUT IN ONE THING THEY WERE SUPERIOR TO ALL THE OTHER CLANS!

WHO OWNS ONE. THE HOKAGE CLAN SCROLL!!

COOL, HUH? I'M THE ONLY PERSON IN JAPAN

THIS SYMBOL ....

HO HO

I'VE SEEN IT ...

SOME-WHERE ...

Fujin
(GOD OF WINDS)

Raijin
(GOD OF THUNDER)

Ensui

?

THAT REALLY IS AMAZING!

WOW...

HUH!?

FUJIN!? ENSUI!?

WHAT'S ALL THIS?!!!

THOSE ARE *THEIR* WORK!!?

FINALLY... I CAN REPAY HER!!

SHE'S STUCK BY ME ALL THESE YEARS...

MY OBSESSION'S BEEN HARD ON HER.

HE TOLD ME FUNDING WOULDN'T BE A PROBLEM.

TEA'S READY

WA P

WA P

STOP HITTING ME

GOOD LUCK, MR. TATESAKO!!

WE NEED HIM *ALIVE*, MOKUREN!!

OUR TARGET IS FUMIO TATESAKO.

K S

S S S H

KUREI'S ORDERS-- OKAY!?

HAVE YOU TAKEN STEPS TO RESOLVE ...

THAT MATTER ?

I'VE SENT KAORU KOGANEI AND MOKUREN NAGAI.

DON'T WORRY, FATHER ....

HE'S A SECURITY RISK...

THAT NEEDS TO BE DEALT WITH.

FUMIO TATESAKO KNOWS TOO MUCH ABOUT THE HOKAGE.

WOOD ....

GOLD AND

KSSSH

HEH HEH... VERY GOOD.

WH·A·P

K·O

HA HA HA

KSSSH

YOU STINK, HANABISHI!! THAT'S MY 61ST WIN!!!

OOKEEE!

BWA HA HHA HA HA

DAMN! I LOST AGAIN!!

IT'S MY FIRST TIME BUT DON'T WORRY!!

I'M MAKING DINNER FOR EVERYBODY TONIGHT!

SO, HANABISHI...

I'M WORRIED.

SAY, THE WOMEN HAVE BEEN OUT SHOPPING A LONG TIME.

HMPH!! I HAVEN'T LOST TO PRINCESS YET, THOUGH.

ONLY BECAUSE SHE DOESN'T KNOW HOW TO DO THE SPECIAL MOVES...

KROOK

I GOT A BAD FEELING!!

WAIT!!!

....! IS IT HIROKO AND SAKOSHITA?

TONK
TONK
TONK

KRK

SHINK...

KRE EEK

ANYBODY HOME?

YOU MUST BE FUMIO TATESAKO.

HEH HEH HEH

HEE HEE

I DON'T.

NO.

?

DO YOU KNOW HIM?

I'LL BE YOUR KIDNAPPER TONIGHT!

NICE TO MEET YOU...

DIDN'T YOUR MOMMA TEACH YOU THAT KIDNAPPING ISN'T POLITE!?

POW

HEY, PUNK!!

KLOMP

KATOU

KLOMP

...

168

NOW WE'RE EVEN!!

BWA-HA-HA-HA! ♪

HANABISHI!!

THAT...

IS...

PUT THAT THING AWAY!

HEY, KID!!

GENKAI DAMA (SHADOW WORLD SPHERE)

Kougon Anki

METAL

(STEEL ASSASSIN INSTRUMENT)

ONE OF THE LEGENDARY HOKAGE CLAN WEAPONS!!

A KŌGON ANKIN!!!

IS THAT THE "BLADE WITH FIVE FACES," FORGED BY ALCHEMY.....

WHERE DID YOU GET THAT !?

IT EXISTS !?

I'LL GIVE YOU A SPANKING !!!

KR KRK

YOU'RE JUST A NAUGHTY BRAT!

KSS...

UNH !?

UNH !?

BABUMP

KILLING'S NO FUN.

I SPRAYED JUST ENOUGH ACONITE TO PARALYZE HIM... HE'LL LIVE.

WHAT PLANT DID YOU USE, MOKUREN?

DON'T TREAT ME LIKE A CHILD.

I'M IN JUNIOR HIGH!

HEE HEE HEE

BONK BONK

HEY, BUDDY!

PARALYZED ... CAN'T MOVE...

HEY, JERKS!

WHAT DO THEY WANT WITH MR. TATE-SAKO!?

GRRN

HE SNIFFED SOME OF THE POWDER, TOO. MAKES OUR JOB EASIER.

UMF

KOGANEI, STOP PLAYING AROUND. LET'S GO.

AWRIGHT ...

DID HE COME TO WHEN HE HEARD HER SCREAM?

LOOKS LIKE HE EVEN STABBED HIMSELF WITH A DAGGER TO...

BREAK THE PARALYSIS!

NO WAY!

SORRY, BUDDY!!

My Picture Diary

HEH-HEH HEH-HEH HEH-HEH **Exculsive Bonus Material--Ultimate Legend**

YOU'RE THE RECCA GROUP LEADER! SHAPE UP!!

I CAN'T SLEEP WITH YOU SNORING!

HEY, ANZAI!!

APPARENTLY MY SNORE IS UNBEARABLE.

HROONK

I'VE GOT TO DO SOMETHING ABOUT IT TO KEEP UP MY WARRIORS' MORALE...OR THEY MIGHT STAGE A COUP D'ETAT...

WHAT SHOULD I DO ....

DEEP THOUGHT

NO ONE EVER TOLD ME I SNORED UNTIL I STARTED WORKING ON "RECCA."

HOW WOULD I KNOW IF I SNORE?

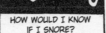

LOOK! HE'S DRINKING AGAIN!

HOW IRRE-SPONSI-BLE!

YELL ALL YOU WANT, BUT I CAN'T HELP IT.

IT'S ONLY PLUM WINE....

HICCUP!

KOTANI? MIKAKO?

IT'S DOMON! IT'S DOMON!

I DISLIKED IT VERY QUICKLY.

FOR THOSE SUFFERING FROM EXCESSIVE SNORING, THIS SUPPOSEDLY WORKS!

THIS IS GREAT!

TA--DA!

SNORE STOPPER!!

JUST PLUG IT INTO YOUR NOSE.

¥2,884

Abrupt New Publication
Magical Girl: Run

◀ **Chapter 1** ▶

BURGLAR
!!

AGE: 13
HOBBY:
PLAYING
THE
TAIKO
DRUM

SWSK

SWSK

La-dee-da
da-dum

TUMP

OH NO
!!

RUN'S
SECRET
IS...

HEY
!

YOU'RE
...

I'LL
CATCH
YOU AND
BURN
YOU! ♡

SHE'S
A
WITCH
!!

FWO

OOSH

181

(I'LL WRITE MORE IF I FEEL LIKE IT.)

Charged with finding seven Celestial Warrior protectors, and given a mission to save her new world, Miaka encounters base villains and dashing heroes — and still manages to worry about where her next banquet is coming from.

VOLUMES
1-11
OUT NOW!

GOLLANCZ MANGA

find out more at www.orionbooks.co.uk

fushigi yûgi ™

Welcome to the wonderfully exciting, funny, and heartfelt tale of Miaka Yûki, a normal high-school girl who is suddenly whisked away into a fictional version of ancient China.

Spooky crimes, baffling robberies, and comic would-be detectives, no crime's too tough to crack for Jimmy! . . . especially not his personal case: to find the mysterious masked men and make them change him back . . . All the clues are here – can you solve the case before Jimmy does?

VOLUMES 1-9 OUT NOW!

GOLLANCZ MANGA

find out more at www.orionbooks.co.uk

CASE CLOSED™

MEET JIMMY KUDO.

Ace high-school student with keen powers of observation, he helps police solve the baffling crimes . . . until, hot on the trial of a suspect, he's accosted and fed a strange chemical which transforms him into a puny grade schooler!

FLAME OF RECCA

Demons, battles, mysteries and excitement abound in the adventures of Recca, Domon, Fuko and Yanagi.

COMPLETE OUR SURVEY AND
LET US KNOW WHAT YOU THINK!

❑ Please do NOT send me information about Gollancz Manga, or other Orion titles, products, news and events, special offers or other information.

Name: _____

Address: _____

Town: _____ County: _____ Postcode: _____

❑ Male ❑ Female   Date of Birth (dd/mm/yyyy): __/__/____
(under 13? Parental consent required)

What race/ethnicity do you consider yourself? (please check one)

❑ Asian   ❑ Black   ❑ Hispanic

❑ White/Caucasian   ❑ Other: _____

Which Gollancz Manga series did you purchase?
❑ Case Closed   ❑ Dragon Ball   ❑ Flame of Recca   ❑ Fushigi Yûgi
❑ Maison Ikkoku   ❑ One Piece   ❑ Rurouni Kenshin   ❑ Yu-Gi-Oh!
❑ Yu-Gi-Oh! Duelist

What other Gollancz Manga series have you tried?
❑ Case Closed   ❑ Dragon Ball   ❑ Flame of Recca   ❑ Fushigi Yûgi
❑ Maison Ikkoku   ❑ One Piece   ❑ Rurouni Kenshin   ❑ Yu-Gi-Oh!
❑ Yu-Gi-Oh! Duelist

How many anime and/or manga titles have you purchased in the last year?
How many were Gollancz Manga titles?

Anime	Manga	GM
❑ None	❑ None	❑ None
❑ 1-4	❑ 1-4	❑ 1-4
❑ 5-10	❑ 5-10	❑ 5-10
❑ 11+	❑ 11+	❑ 11+

Reason for purchase: (check all that apply)

❑ Special Offer   ❑ Favourite title   ❑ Gift

❑ In store promotion If so please indicate which store: _____

❑ Recommendation   ❑ Other _____

Where did you make your purchase?

❑ Bookshop   ❑ Comic Shop   ❑ Music Store

❑ Newsagent   ❑ Video Game Store   ❑ Supermarket

❑ Other: _____   ❑ Online: _____

What kind of manga would you like to read?

❑ Adventure   ❑ Comic Strip   ❑ Fantasy

❑ Fighting   ❑ Horror   ❑ Mystery

❑ Romance   ❑ Science Fiction   ❑ Sports

❑ Other: _____

Which do you prefer?

❑ Sound effects in English

❑ Sound effects in Japanese with English captions

❑ Sound effects in Japanese only with a glossary at the back

Want to find out more about Manga?

Look it up at www.orionbooks.co.uk, or www.viz.com

THANK YOU!

Please send the completed form to:

Manga Survey
Orion Books
Orion House
5 Upper St Martin's Lane
London, WC2H 9EA